Contents

Introduction

Tennis is the most popular of all the racket sports. It is played on an area called a 'court'. Its official name is 'lawn tennis', but there are other court surfaces as well as grass, such as cement, clay and tarmac (outdoors), rubberized carpet (indoors) and artificial grass (inside and out).

The object in tennis is to knock a ball over a net and into your opponent's half of the court so that your opponent cannot get it back or makes a mistake. You may hit the ball before it has bounced or after one bounce. Tennis is played as singles, one against one, or doubles, two against two.

▽ The big tennis tournaments attract huge crowds and the leading players earn fortunes. The French Championships (shown here) are played on clay courts.

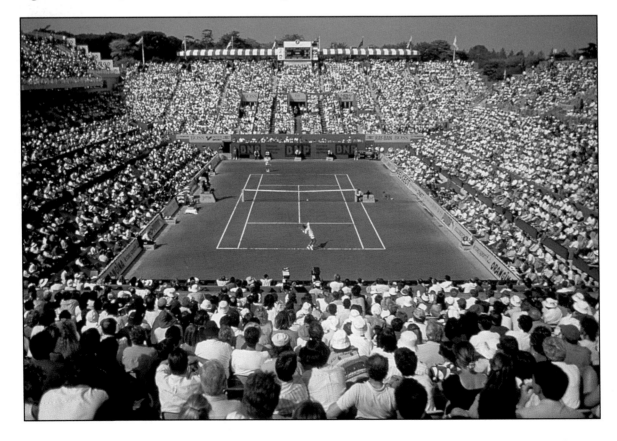

▷ Short tennis helps you to learn tennis strokes without too much effort. The player here is about to hit a 'backhand' shot - the back of his racket hand is facing the ball. 'Forehand' strokes are played on the other side of the body, on the right for a right-handed player, on the left for a left-handed player.

Once you start playing tennis, you soon want to improve. You need a good eye for the ball, co-ordination of movement, control of different types of shot, or 'stroke', and quickness of foot.

Some of these are natural gifts, but you can develop tennis skills with practice. When young players start, they might find the racket too heavy and the balls difficult to control. It is better to begin with 'short tennis'. This is played on a smaller court, with lighter and shorter rackets, and soft, light balls. It is an easy way to develop strokes and other skills, and it's great fun.

Getting started 1

Not all schools have their own tennis courts, but you can get started in other ways. Many sports centres and tennis clubs have junior sections, some with short tennis, and there are public tennis courts in parks. In some places, there are junior tennis clubs, where you can be taught by a qualified coach.

Balls and rackets may be available for hire where you play. But it is a good idea to have your own racket. It is important when you start that you feel comfortable with your racket. Make sure the weight of the racket and the thickness of the handle feel right.

Tennis involves a lot of running, twisting and turning, often on a hard surface. So tennis shoes should be light and comfortable and provide support as you move around the court. They should have an under-surface that provides a good grip. It helps to wear sports socks with reinforced soles.

Footwear

It is worth getting a good pair of tennis shoes that will support your feet and provide good grip. But there is no need to spend a lot of money on fancy footwear with a 'designer' name, especially if your feet are still growing.

1 Achilles tendon protector
2 Toecap
3 Insock
4 Insole
5 Sole unit (non-marking soles for indoor play)

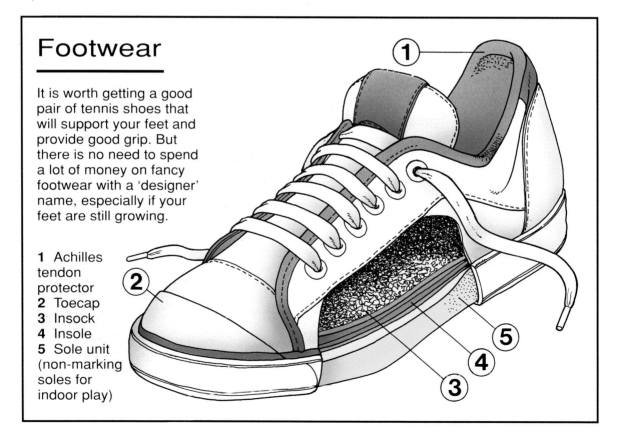

The right racket

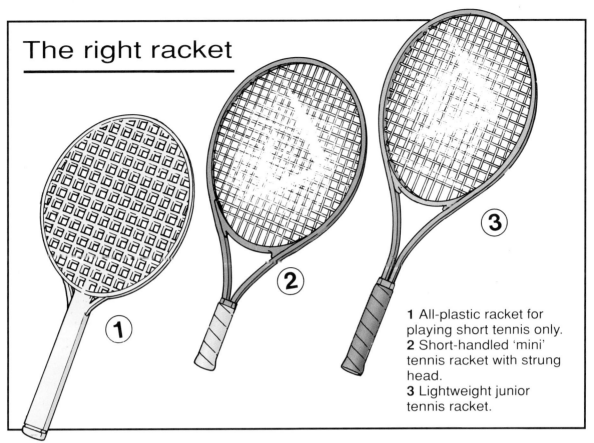

1 All-plastic racket for playing short tennis only.
2 Short-handled 'mini' tennis racket with strung head.
3 Lightweight junior tennis racket.

△ Some clubs provide coaching for beginners.

Getting started 2

The grip, the way you hold your racket, is most important in tennis. There is more than one type of grip, depending on what stroke you are playing. The two basic grips are forehand and backhand. It might seem awkward at first to have to change your grip as you play. But only a slight adjustment is needed, and it makes all the difference between a good shot and a bad one.

The forehand grip is used for forehand groundstrokes (shots played after the ball has bounced) and volleys (shots played without allowing the ball to bounce). The backhand grip is used for backhand groundstrokes and volleys. A central grip (between forehand and backhand) is used for overhead shots. Another common grip is the two-handed backhand, used for certain backhand groundstrokes.

▽ Basic grips, shown for right-handed players. The central grip (not shown) may be used for volleys when there is no time to change the grip, and for overhead shots.
1 The forehand grip. This is sometimes called the 'shake hands' grip, because you grasp the racket as if you are shaking someone's hand.
2 The backhand grip. Note how the palm of the hand has moved round to be on top of the handle.
3 Two-handed backhand grip. The left hand joins the right hand, which is using the normal backhand grip.

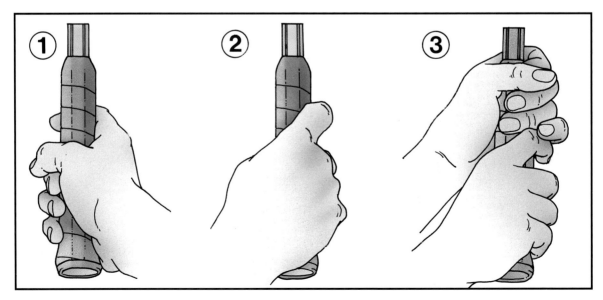

Short tennis is the best way to learn how to play tennis. You might be able to play short tennis at school, or you could go to a club where they have short tennis. If not, it is worth getting some equipment. Rackets and spongy balls are not expensive. You can play with a friend, hitting the ball to each other. Or you can practise by yourself against a wall.

The object of short tennis is to give yourself an easy introduction to the full-size game. It is much easier to control the ball in short tennis.

The gradual steps from short tennis to the proper game are: First change to 'transition' balls, which are livelier than foam ones. Then change from a plastic racket to a strung junior or mini racket. Progress to a proper tennis court, with the net lowered and perhaps using only the service areas (see page 11). Build up to a full-size court and a racket more suited to your size. Finally, use proper tennis balls.

△ An indoor short-tennis school, with spectators and scoreboard painted on the backcloth. The age range for playing short tennis is from about 5 to 9 years old.

Rules and scoring 1

Tennis rules are simple. The court is marked out as shown opposite. The side areas are used only for doubles play.

Each point, or rally, is started with a service. On the first point of a game, service is from the right of the little white mark on the centre of the baseline. You serve over the net and into your opponent's right-hand service court. Your opponent must let the ball bounce, and then return it into any part of your court. The rally continues until one player fails to return the ball into his or her opponent's court. For the next point, service is from the left-hand of the baseline into the opponent's left-hand service court, and so on. The same player serves until a 'game' is over. Then the other player serves.

▽ A player prepares to serve, with a spare ball in his pocket in case he needs it for a second service. Players are allowed two services each time. A 'fault' is called if a service goes into the net or otherwise fails to land in the correct service court. If both serves are faults - a 'double fault' - the server loses that point.

The court

A tennis court, showing the service courts. The side areas are not part of the court in singles. The net projects out on either side of the court. Note that the net is higher at the ends (107 cm) than in the middle (91 cm).

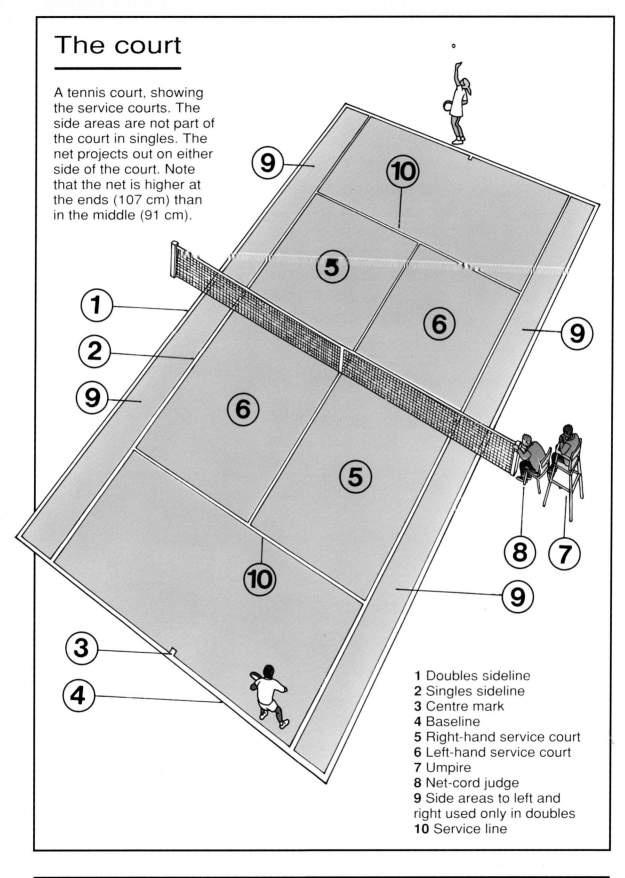

1 Doubles sideline
2 Singles sideline
3 Centre mark
4 Baseline
5 Right-hand service court
6 Left-hand service court
7 Umpire
8 Net-cord judge
9 Side areas to left and right used only in doubles
10 Service line

Rules and scoring 2

You need to win at least four points to win a game. In tennis, the points go from 0 (called 'love'), to 15, for your first point, 30, 40 and 'game'. If both players have three points, 40-40, it is called 'deuce'. This is like going back to 30-30, because you cannot win the game until you are two points ahead. After deuce, the next player to win a point is said to have 'advantage', 'A' on the scoreboard. If that player wins the next point, he or she wins the game. If not, the score goes back to deuce.

   You need at least six games to win a 'set', but you must be two games ahead. If a set reaches 6-6, you play a tie-breaker.

▽ A net-cord judge sits with his finger on the net and a ball-boy waits at the ready during a tournament game. For competitive matches, there is an umpire, who sits on a high chair and is helped by line judges. They call when a ball is hit out of court. The net-cord judge calls 'let' when a service hits the top of the net and goes over. If the ball then falls in the correct service court, the service is played again.

▷ Good teamwork is important in doubles. You try not to go for the same ball, or both leave the ball to each other. In this ladies' doubles, the player at the back has managed to retrieve a shot that her partner closer to the net has been unable to reach.

You change ends after the first game of a set and then after every two games.

The doubles game is played on the whole court, but the service areas are the same. Service games alternate between sides as in singles. The same player serves for one game, and then his or her partner serves the next time that side has service. A pair may change their order of serving for each set. The player who starts receiving service from the right-hand court must continue to do so throughout the set. After service and return of service, either player may play the ball. The players may move around the court as they like.

In tennis, a ball that hits one of the lines bounding the court, the baseline or sideline, is called 'in'. In the same way, a service hitting a service line is in. Some calls are difficult for an umpire or line judge to make. Never argue with a call. Bad calls tend to even out over a match. When playing without an umpire or line judges, always make honest calls.

Groundstrokes 1

Groundstrokes are the first skills you learn at tennis. They are what you build your game on. Whether playing on the forehand or the backhand, you aim to strike the ball at a comfortable distance from your body so that you can make a good swing with your racket.

The drives are fairly 'flat' shots, made with the racket square on to the ball, as shown in figure 4 in the sequences below. But you can also use backspin or topspin by angling your racket as you hit the ball.

▷ Argentinian star Gabriela Sabatini takes her racket back as she prepares to make a forehand drive.

Forehand drive

1 The ready position.
2 Begin to take the racket back early.
3 Make a smooth change from backswing to forward swing.
4 Step into the shot, moving your weight on to your leading foot, and hitting the ball slightly forward of your leading hip.
5 Follow through with racket swinging up.

Backhand drive

1 The ready position.
2 Using the left hand for support, change to the backhand grip.
3 On the backswing, again support the racket with your other hand.
4 Move your weight onto your leading foot as you step into the shot.
5 Follow through with racket swinging up.

Groundstrokes 2

The drives are attacking shots, particularly if you use topspin. You do this by angling your racket over the top of the ball. A well-placed topspin drive deep into your opponent's court puts him or her under extra pressure because of its fast, high bounce.

The opposite spin is backspin, or 'slice'. Angling your racket underneath the ball produces slice. It is easier to control the ball with a sliced shot, particularly on the backhand. It is a good defensive stroke because you can play it quickly and still make an accurate, deep return.

◁ Steffi Graf of Germany takes her racket back to play a sliced backhand.

Young players often use a two-handed backhand because they need an extra hand to control the racket on that side.

The big disadvantage of the two-handed technique is that it cuts down a player's reach. But if your footwork is good enough to get into position to play the shot, it can be a powerful attacking weapon. And if you feel comfortable with it, there is no reason why you should not adopt this style.

Some of the world's leading players, both men and women, use the two-handed backhand. It is very effective when an opponent has come up to the net. Two-handed players can disguise their shots so that the net player cannot tell until the last moment where the ball is going.

△ The two-handed backhand gives extra control and power. But you need to get into position quickly, or you might find yourself reaching for the ball off balance.

Volleying

Most volleys are played from close to the net, so you have less time to position yourself for the shot. You need a quick eye for volleying and the ability to judge where your opponent will hit the ball. The best way to attack and to make winning shots is with a volley. In volleying, the backswing is much shorter than for groundstrokes. You play the ball with a blocking, punching action, with no follow-through.

Good volleying calls for confidence more than anything else. The best way to achieve this is to make volleying a regular part of your practice. Get your practice partner to drive balls to you at the net so that you can improve both forehand and backhand volleys.

Forehand volley

1 The ready position.
2 Get feet and racket into position early and take only a short backswing.
3 With slightly bent arm, aim to play the ball a comfortable distance to the side of your body.
4 Stepping into the shot, move your weight on to your leading foot as you make contact.

Backhand volley

1 The ready position.
2 Prepare early and support the racket in your other hand as you take the short backswing.
3 Aim to play the ball a comfortable distance to the side, with slightly bent arm.
4 Transfer your weight on to your leading foot as you step into the shot.

△ Australian Pat Cash prepares to make a low forehand volley. If you have to play a ball dipping below the height of the net, you need to angle your racket slightly upwards.

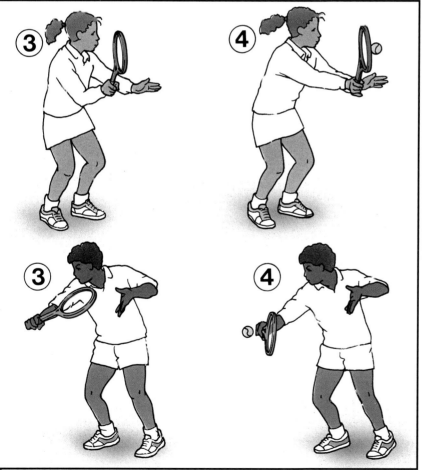

Overhead shots

A strong, consistent service is a great asset in tennis. Practise getting your action right before hitting the ball too hard. Build up a routine, starting with the throw, which is very important. Keep well balanced throughout. The hitting action is like throwing a ball very hard.

When the ball is played back high, you can hit it with an overhead shot, or 'smash', at the highest point of your reach. The smash is often an outright winner, especially if you are close to the net. The action is similar to the service. The important things are good timing and correct positioning of your feet.

▽ **1** Standing behind the baseline, with feet sideways on to the line, support your racket with your other hand.
2 Throw the ball smoothly into the air at a comfortable height above your head, at the same time drawing your racket back behind you.
3 and **4** Bring your racket up and the racket head back and down for extra power, ready to hit the ball.
5 'Throw' the racket head at the ball as it drops, hitting it at full height and slightly in front of you.
6 Follow through in the direction of the ball, ready to make your next shot.

The service

△ Some players use a high throw when serving, striking the ball as it begins to drop.

Other shots

As your tennis progresses, you will realize that there are all kinds of shots you can make to outwit your opponent. You can hit a 'lob', a shot played up and over an opponent at the net. You can play a 'half-volley', striking the ball as it bounces up from the court. Or you can do a 'drop-shot', hitting the ball so that it drops just over the net.

Tactics are an important part of tennis, and you will learn to vary your shots to make them more difficult for your opponent to return. With experience, you will learn where to place the ball and when to use power or spin. To play really well, you also need to be fit and to develop speed around the court and accuracy with your shots.

△ This is a delicate little shot that calls for perfect control. Pat Cash has taken the ball on the half-volley, hitting it as it bounces, and has played a drop-shot, sending the ball just over the net so that it drops down on the other side, out of reach of his opponent.

The lob

▽ When an opponent is at the net, instead of trying to drive the ball wide on either side, you might play a lob, over your opponent's head.

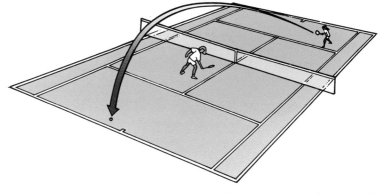

△ Lobs are usually played from near the back of the court. You aim to lift the ball up and out of reach of your opponent, so that it lands near the baseline.

Half-volleys

Half-volleys are strokes, backhand or forehand, played just after the ball touches the ground. They call for perfect timing. Half-volleys are usually played when you are approaching the net.

▷ Stefan Edberg of Sweden gets down to make a half-volley.

Drop-shots

Drop-shots are useful strokes to play when your opponent is near the baseline. You hit the ball with backspin so that it drops just over the net and takes your opponent by surprise.

1 The sliced drop-shot, played off a bouncing ball.
2 The 'stop volley' is played with an angled racket, which is 'stopped' rather than punched through the ball.

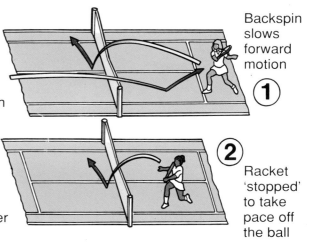

Backspin slows forward motion

①

② Racket 'stopped' to take pace off the ball

Positioning

You adopt the 'ready position', as illustrated earlier in some of the strokes, before you make your shots. The object of the ready position is to be prepared to move in any direction and make any shot. You stand loosely on the balls of your feet, legs apart, with racket held slightly up in front of you and pointing towards the net.

When receiving serve, you have plenty of time to take up the ready position. During a rally, you do the best you can. If you are playing from the back, you try to get back to the middle of the baseline or just behind it after each return. When volleying, you aim to cover as much of the net as possible from about two or three paces behind it.

◁ The ready position allows you to spring off in any direction to make a return. Note the knees slightly bent, free hand supporting the racket and body bent over towards the racket head.

▷ Positioning is an important part of learning. Coaches try to teach you good habits when you first start to play, so that they soon come naturally.

Fitness and warming up

Playing tennis to a good standard calls for a high degree of fitness. Rallies between well-matched players often last for several strokes, especially if played from the baselines. When you first take up the game, just playing tennis is enough to keep you fit. But if you want to play seriously and enter tournaments, you will need to follow a programme of fitness training.

However fit you are, it is essential to do warming-up exercises before strenuous practice or playing a match. You need to prepare your muscles for the stress that running, twisting and hitting puts on them.

△ Boris Becker of Germany demonstrates the kind of agility needed to play tennis at the very top level. Becker started playing very early and was a junior champion. He won the world's top tournament, the Wimbledon Singles Championship, when only 17 years old, the youngest player ever to do so.

Stretching exercises

1 Calf muscles With feet flat on the ground, lean forward, with the back knee straight. Change legs.

2 Groin muscles With one knee bent, stretch the other out sideways. Change legs.

3 Thigh muscles Balancing on one leg, bend the other leg up, holding the ankle. Change legs.

4 Hamstrings (back of thigh) Clasp your ankle with both hands, keeping legs straight. Change legs.

5 Trunk side-bends With feet apart, bend from side to side, swinging each arm over your head.

6 Back Clasping your hands in front of your body, stretch them over your head and back as far as you can.

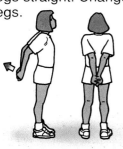

7 Back Clasping your hands together behind your back, extend them as far as you can.

8 Shoulders With arms outstretched, make large circular swings, forwards and backwards.

9 Neck With shoulders still, stretch your head and neck up and down, then from side to side.

Warming-up exercises might take from 5 to 15 minutes. Probably 7 or 8 minutes is enough to start with, building up to 15 minutes as you get stronger.

You should divide your warming-up sessions into three parts. Begin with 3 minutes of gentle jogging. Then do some stretching exercises, as shown here. Stretch the muscles smoothly.

Never bounce or jerk. Do each exercise for a minimum of 5 seconds, repeated three to five times.

Lastly, for no more than 3 minutes, do some really 'explosive' exercises. These could include short sprints, star jumps and running backwards and sideways. Make sure you take a rest between each exercise.

Competition

In many countries, there are coaching schools for helping young players. You are first taught the strokes in short tennis. Coaching continues as you progress to junior tennis. It is important, if you want to improve, to be coached by qualified people. They will correct faults in your play and help you develop your skills.

You can enter short tennis competitions at the age of about 8 or 9. As you get older, there are junior tennis competitions for various age groups, starting with 10 and under and going up to 16.

△ At a 'fun morning' organized during the Wimbledon Championships, top coaches and players mingle with young players to give them tips and encourage them to learn and enjoy the game.

In some countries, there is a system of junior tennis ratings. You are first graded by a coach, who gives you a rating number. When you enter special ratings tournaments, your results go into a computer, which then adjusts your rating according to how well you do. It is a good measure of your progress.

△ Some tennis players reach the top level while still in their teens. American star Jennifer Capriati was competing with the world's best players when she was 13 years old, and won the 1992 Olympic Games women's singles title at the age of 16.

Glossary

Advantage
Needing the next point to win a game after 'deuce'.

Backhand
The left-hand side for right-handed players (right for left-handers).

Baselines
The lines marked at each end of the court.

Deuce
When the players' scores in a game are at 40-40.

Drives
The basic strokes of tennis, played with either the forehand or the backhand and usually from near the back of the court after the ball has bounced.

Drop-shot
A shot played to land just over the net.

Fault
A service that does not land in the correct service court.

Forehand
The right-hand side for a right-handed player (left for left-handers).

Game
A group of points played as part of a set. The first player to win four points with a lead of at least two wins the game. See also Set; Advantage; Deuce.

Groundstrokes
Shots played after the ball has bounced.

Half-volley
A shot played close to the ground after the bounce.

Let
Any instance when a point must be played again, such as when a service hits the net cord and falls into the correct court.

Lob
A shot played up in the air and over your opponent.

Net cord
The tape at the top of the net.

Overhead strokes
Shots played with your racket stretched out above your head.

Rally
The play back and forth over the net for a point.

Ready position
The way you stand as you prepare to receive a shot.

Service
The act of putting the ball into play at the start of each point.

Set
A group of games played as part of a match. The first player to win six games (with a lead of at least two games), wins the set. In most matches, the first player to win two sets is the winner (best of three sets). Men sometimes play the best of five sets.

Short tennis
A game for young beginners, from about 5 years old up to 9.

Slice
A shot played by angling the racket under the ball.

Smash
An overhead shot hit hard into your opponent's court.

Tie-breaker
A game with special scoring used in most competitions to decide a set that has reached the score 6-6. Players change service after the first point and then every two points, and the first to seven points (with a two-point lead) wins the game (and the set 7-6).

Topspin
A shot played by angling the racket over the top of the ball.

Volleys
Shots played without allowing the ball to bounce in your court.

Books to read

Step by Step Tennis Skills, Deutscher Tennis Bund (Hamlyn, 1988)
Take up Tennis, Anne Pankhurst (Springfield Books, 1987)
Tennis, Charles Applewhaite and Bill Moss (Crowood Press, 1987)
Tennis (Know the Game series), LTA (A & C Black, 1991)
Tennis (How to Play series), Mike Shaw (Jarrold, 1989)

For teachers and coaches:
Elementary Coaches Handbook, Charles Applewhaite (LTA Trust, 1989)
How to Coach Tennis, Bill Moss (Willow Books, 1990)

Index